FAVORITE PATCHWORK PATTERNS

Full–Size Templates and Instructions for 12 Quilts

Henry Louis Pelletier

Dover Publications, Inc., New York

Published in Canada by General Publishing Company, Ltd., 30 Lesmill Road, Don Mills, Toronto, Ontario.
Published in the United Kingdom by Constable and Company, Ltd., 10 Orange Street, London WC2H 7EG.

Favorite Patchwork Patterns: Full-Size Templates and Instructions for 12 Quilts is a new work, first published by Dover Publications, Inc., in 1984.

Manufactured in the United States of America
Dover Publications, Inc., 31 East 2nd Street, Mineola, N.Y. 11501

Library of Congress Cataloging in Publication Data

Pelletier, Henry Louis.
  Favorite patchwork patterns.

  1. Quilting—Patterns. 2. Patchwork—Patterns.
I. Title. II. Series.
TT835.P43 1984   746.9'7041   84-6087
ISBN 0-486-24753-8 (pbk.)

INTRODUCTION

The twelve patterns in this book represent the most beautiful designs for patchwork that I have found after a long and exhaustive search through thousands of contemporary and traditional patterns.

Many pattern books limit their tonal ranges to two or three colors. While this might be sufficient to portray, through contrast, the basic geometry of a patchwork design, I feel that the more complex beauty of a well-orchestrated six-color quilt is far superior and well within the grasp of anyone who can follow a simple diagram.

For each quilt in this book, I have provided specifications of the quilt size and arrangement of blocks and borders. A table indicates the number of pieces of fabric to be cut for each shape and color, and the amount of 45-inch material needed for each type of piece. A diagram of a single block is keyed to the table by number. A complete shaded diagram shows the effect of the contrasting colors in the assembled quilt. Exact-size templates on heavy paper for each pattern make it easy to cut out the shapes with precision.

Remember that careful planning and design will increase the beauty of your quilt and reward your diligent craftsmanship with breathtaking beauty and lasting satisfaction.

HENRY LOUIS PELLETIER

INSTRUCTIONS

As the title indicates, this work is primarily a collection of immediately useable patterns—not a complete instruction book on how to do patchwork; that subject is already well covered in numerous inexpensive books (one of the best of which is *The Standard Book of Quilt Making and Collecting* by Marguerite Ickis [Dover 20582-7]), and limitations of space permit us only to sketch out the process in brief.

BEGINNING THE QUILT

Before cutting out the pieces for an entire quilt, always make one block of the pattern. This gives you a chance to double-check your pattern and to make certain that you like both the pattern and the color choices.

Cutting Out the Pattern Pieces

All of the pattern pieces used in making these quilts are given in actual-size patterns or templates printed on heavy paper in the back of this book. Locate the designated template and carefully cut it out. Use this cardboard template to make your sample block. If you decide to make the entire quilt, you may want to mount your template on heavier cardboard, sandpaper or plastic.

It is important that all templates be cut out carefully because, if they are not accurate, the patchwork pieces will not fit together. Use a pair of good-size sharp scissors, a single-edged razor blade or an X-ACTO knife. Be careful not to bend the fine corners of the triangles.

Kinds of Materials

At the beginning of each pattern, we indicate the amount of 45-inch-wide material you will need to complete a quilt of the specified dimensions. Of course, you are free to revise the proposed finished size of the quilt. This adjustment is accomplished by adding additional blocks or half-blocks to the width and/or the height.

The first rule to observe in selecting material for a quilt is to combine the same kinds of fabrics. For instance, linens and cottons go together, silks and satins, and so on. If you want to make a quilt that can be laundered, be sure that *all* the material used is washable and pre-shrunk and that the colors are fast.

For your convenience in sewing, select a soft material, not too closely woven. Closely woven cloth makes the needlework more difficult and is no stronger than thinner goods. Materials that are stiff because of being "treated" with a finish are also difficult to work with. In general, the following materials are good for patchwork quilts: gingham, percale, calico, shirting, broadcloth, and cotton-polyester blends.

Cutting the Fabric

Cutting is one of the most important steps in making your quilt. You must be accurate in order to have the pattern fit perfectly and to avoid wasting your materials. Have sharp scissors with blades at least 4 inches long. You will need a ruler for marking straight lines, and a pencil with hard lead to avoid blurry marks around the pattern.

Press all fabric to remove the wrinkles and crease marks. Check the grain line of the fabric carefully. Lengthwise threads should be parallel to the selvage and crosswise threads exactly perpendicular to the selvage to insure that the pieces will be correctly cut.

Take one of the templates and refer to the diagram for that pattern to determine how many pieces of each fabric you will need to complete your first sample block. For convenience you may wish to write on each pattern piece the total number of that piece to be cut out in each color.

These templates are the exact size the patch will be after the sewing is done, and they have purposely been printed *without* the ¼-inch seam allowance. Lay the cardboard template on the wrong side of the fabric near the top edge of the material (but not on the selvage) placing it so as many straight sides of the pattern as possible are parallel to the crosswise and lengthwise grain of the fabric.

Trace around the cardboard with a well-sharpened, hard lead pencil. Now measure ¼ inch around this shape. Using a ruler, draw this second line. This is the line you will cut on. Now you will see that the first line (where you traced the template) is there to use as a guide for stitching. If the seam allowance is not perfect, this will not show; but the *sewing line* must be perfectly straight and true, or the pieces will not fit together into a perfectly shaped design.

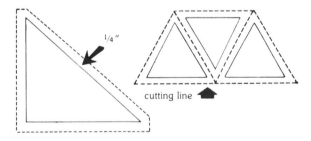

The broken line is the cutting line. The solid line is the seam line; match to the line on the next patch. Sewing is done on the solid line. The pieces can share a common cutting line.

Continue moving the template and tracing it on the fabric the required number of times, moving from left to right and always keeping the straight sides parallel with the grain. As each piece is traced, add the ¼ inch around it before going on to the next piece. You will save fabric if you have the pieces share a common cutting line, but if this is confusing leave a narrow border or margin around each piece.

After you have traced the first pattern piece the required number of times, take one of the other pattern pieces that is to be cut from the same material, and trace it in a similar matter, referring to the specifications printed for each quilt to determine the required number of pieces.

Run thread through center of patches according to shape and color. Knot at bottom and lift off patch from top as needed.

Carefully cut out all of the pieces of each color and then organize them according to shape and color. Most people find it convenient to keep the pieces of the same shape and color together by putting them in a pile and running a thread with a knot in one end through the center. Each piece is then lifted off as it is needed.

Sewing the Block

Before beginning to sew one block, lay out all of the pieces that will be needed for that block. Always work with well-ironed fabric; all pieces should be ironed before they are sewn together. Use a short needle, #7 to #10 (sizes #9 and #10 are the most popular), and an 18-inch length of #60 thread. Try various needles until you find the one that is most comfortable for you. A long needle is not necessary because you are taking only a few stitches at a time, and a short needle is much easier to work with. Use white thread unless the patches are cut from very dark cloth.

To join two pieces, place them together with the right sides facing. Place a pin through both pieces at each end of the pencil line. Check on the back to make sure that the pins are *exactly* on the pencil lines. When sewing larger seams, place a pin every 1½ inches, removing pins as you sew past them. Always stitch on the sewing line, being very careful not to stitch into the margins at the corners.

Join the pieces with short, simple running stitches,

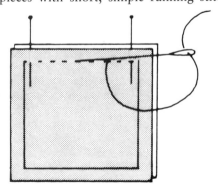

Place a pin through both pieces at each end of the pencil line.

Do not stitch into the margins at the corners.

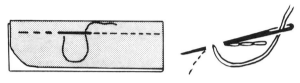

Running stitch.   *Back stitch.*

taking a few back stitches at the beginning and end of each seam rather than a knot. If the seam is very long, it is a good idea to make a few back stitches at several places along the seam. Keep the seam as straight as possible along the pencil line. If you must sew two bias edges together, try to keep the thread taut enough so that the edges do not stretch as you sew them.

After you join two pieces together, press the seams flat to one side—not open. Open seams will weaken the quilt. Generally seams should all be pressed in the same direction, but darker pieces should not be pressed so that they fall under the lighter pieces since they may show through when the quilt is completed. All seams should be pressed before they are crossed with another seam. To keep seams from bunching, clip away excess fabric, if necessary, at these crossing points.

As for using a sewing machine, old-time quilters frown on anything but the finest hand sewing when piecing blocks. However, the sewing machine can serve a useful purpose when you are ready to set the blocks together—more about this below.

Setting the Quilt

After you have pieced the required number of blocks, lay them out to get the final effect before setting them together. Check to make sure that each block is turned the proper way.

You can now proceed with setting the blocks together. The best way is to join all the blocks of one row, sewing them with a ¼-inch seam. Continue joining blocks one row at a time. Some people feel that machine sewing here not only saves time but also strengthens the long seams. Others believe that it is easier to keep the pattern accurate and the corners matched if the work is done by hand. Some hand sewers also find that the close machine stitches create difficulties later on when one gets ready to do the final quilt stitching.

Blocking the Quilt

The term "blocking" means keeping the edges straight on all sides of the quilt so that it will be a perfect rectangle when finished. The term applies to the quilt's divisions as well as to the entire quilt, so the process of blocking is a continuous process from start to finish.

Right at the start it will help the blocking process if you have cut all of your pieces with the straight sides of the pattern parallel to the grain of the fabric, because pieces cut on the bias have a tendency to pucker.

Pull the edges of the block straight with the fingers and pin the corners to the ironing board to hold them rigidly in place. Cover the block with a damp cloth and steam with a warm iron. Do not let the pressing cloth get dry. Iron the edges until they are perfectly straight and of equal measurements. The center is ironed last.

It is a good idea to iron each block after the sewing is completed. This means quite a lot of ironing, but it assures greater accuracy in the final measurements of all units. After the quilt is set together, it will need a final blocking before it is ready to be quilted to the filling and lining.

FINISHING THE QUILT

A completed quilt consists of three parts: the patchwork top, the filler or batting and the lining. The quilting stitches are used to firmly lock the patchwork top to both the lining and the batting in the middle. In primitive times, the three layers of covering were held together by stitches at a few main points, called the counter points. Next came interlacing diagonal lines, forming squares and diamonds, and gradually the decorative quilt stitching that we generally associate with early American quilts.

When the quilt is composed of squares, the quilting stitches cover the plain squares, which alternate with the decorated ones, and this gives the effect of throwing the decorated part into more pronounced relief. These quilting stitches in the plain squares are sometimes in straight or diagonal lines and are usually planned to form a contrast to the pieced blocks. Thus, straight lines are chosen to contrast with a curving design, and curves and whirls are chosen when the main pattern is straight or geometrical.

Quilt Lining and Batting

You should choose the lining and batting for your quilt with the greatest care if you want your quilt to endure for years. It is false economy to use inferior materials; all of your time and painstaking stitches deserve the best! You may obtain cotton batting that is especially prepared for quilt filling. It comes in large sheets carefully folded and rolled. Perhaps you will need two packages, depending on the size of the quilt.

The back of the quilt is made of lengths of soft material

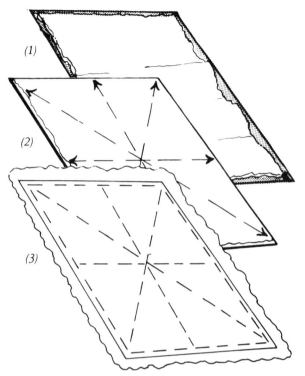

Finishing the quilt. (1) Placing batting on lining. (2) Basting batting to lining. (3) Basting marked top to batting and lining, through center and around edges.

sewn together for correct width and length. It should be soft and loosely woven to make the quilt stitching easier. The overall measurements should be 2 inches longer on each side to allow for binding when the quilt is completed. Carefully arrange the lining on a large flat surface, and fasten the corners with thumbtacks. Unroll the cotton batting and spread it out evenly on the lining, making sure there are no lumps or thin places that will make the quilting uneven.

Next, fasten the cotton batting securely to the lining with long basting stitches. Start in the center of the quilt, and sew toward the edge until you have a number of diagonal lines, as shown above.

Preparing the Quilt Top

Before the quilt top is joined to the batting and lining, the quilting pattern must be marked on the quilt top. There are many methods for marking the design on the fabric. The easiest method is to use a hard lead pencil. If the material is dark, use chalk or a piece of white soap trimmed to a thin point. If you sew directly on the pencil or chalk lines, they will not show when the work is finished.

You are now ready to lay the neatly ironed top in place over the lining and the cotton filling. Smooth it out and see that the edges correspond on all four sides. The three layers are now basted together just as you basted the first two—in diagonal lines from the center to the edges of the quilt.

The Quilting Stitch

The actual quilt stitching is a simple process for anyone who can do any other form of needlework, but it does take a little practice. The first attempt should be in stitching straight lines, with curves and feathers coming later. It is helpful to use a practice piece of two squares of material with a layer of cotton in between. Try stitching the pieces together with a plain running stitch. You will soon learn the best method of pushing the needle in and out, and also the direction in which to sew. You will be sure to find that it is easier to sew *toward* you.

It is an interesting fact that many busy women who enjoy piecing blocks, but who do not care for the final quilting of the three layers, procure the services of professional quilters. There are church organizations, craft shops and private seamstresses who accept quilting at fair rates.

One reason why quilt stitching is often "farmed out" is that it is greatly simplified when done on a quilting frame, which is cumbersome. However, quilting can also be done successfully, if less rapidly, on a quilting hoop.

The purpose of the quilting stitch is to firmly lock the top of the quilt to both its filling and lining. Use a short sharp needle, size #8 to #9. The choice of thread should be between #50 and #70, preferably white. It is important to start the quilting near the center of the frame because it is always easier to sew toward the body. To commence, make a knot at the end of the thread and bring the needle through to the top of the quilt, then pull gently but firmly and the knot will slip through the lower layer into the padding where it will not be seen. To finish off, make a single back stitch and run the thread through the padding. Cut, and the end will be lost.

Binding the Quilt

When the quilting is completed, trim the edges (except the lining extension if used for binding) on all four sides in an even line, being sure to remove any cotton that extends beyond the quilt's top. There are two methods for binding the edges: (1) Make use of the 2-inch extension of the back lining which was left on during the quilting process. Even it off all around, turn up an edge for a seam, and fold up over the top of the quilt. Sew in place with small hemming stitches in matching color thread. (2) Bind the edges with bias strips, if you are going to use a binding of different color or a scalloped border. Cut the bias strips 1 inch wide and sew them together. The binding is done by laying the bias strip along the outside edge of the quilt, and fitting the edges together so they match exactly. Sew the bias strip and all three layers together with a ¼-inch seam, using a running stitch. After the sewing is done, turn the quilt over and turn down the edges of the bias strip ¼ inch. Fold this over the back of the quilt and sew securely to the bottom layer with small hemming stitches.

FAVORITE PATCHWORK PATTERNS

Roman Stripe Quilt

SIZE OF QUILT

This quilt, measuring 80″ × 104″, is made up of forty-eight 12-inch pieced blocks set six in width and eight in length with a 4-inch border.

NUMBER OF PIECES TO BE CUT   AMOUNT OF MATERIAL

Piece No. 1 96	1 yard
Piece No. 2 96	1 yard
Piece No. 3 96	1 yard
Piece No. 4 96	1 yard
Piece No. 5 96	1 yard
Piece No. 6 96	1 yard

(Border pieces)
Two strips 4½″ × 80½″   1½ yards
Two strips 4½″ × 96½″

(Backing)
Two pieces 40½″ × 104½″   6 yards

COLOR CHART

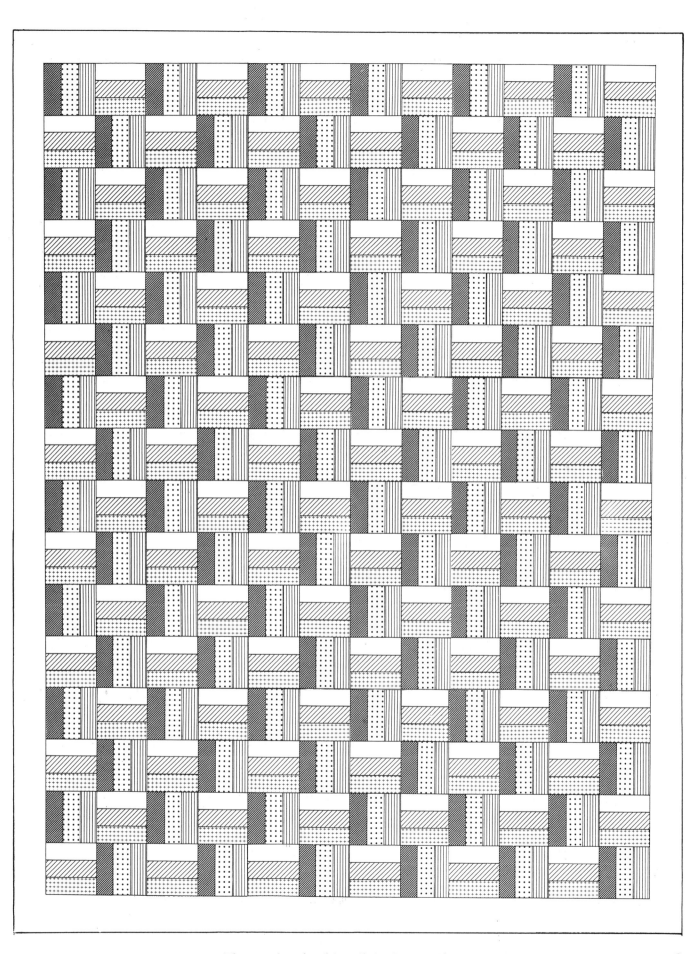

The template for this quilt is given on Plate 1.

Lafayette Orange Peel Quilt

SIZE OF QUILT

This quilt, measuring 80″ × 98″, is made up of eighty 9-inch pieced blocks set eight in width and ten in length with a 4-inch border.

NUMBER OF PIECES TO BE CUT	AMOUNT OF MATERIAL
Piece No. 1 80	1½ yards
Piece No. 2 80	1½ yards
Piece No. 3 80	1½ yards
Piece No. 4 80	1½ yards
(Continuous background) Two pieces 40½″ × 96½	6 yards
(Border pieces) Two strips 4½″ × 80½″ Two strips 4½″ × 90½″	1½ yards
(Backing pieces) Two pieces 40½″ × 98½″	6 yards

Note that the entire background is made up of 9-inch squares that can be cut into individual pieces or treated as a single piece. The numbered pieces are appliquéd onto the background.

COLOR CHART

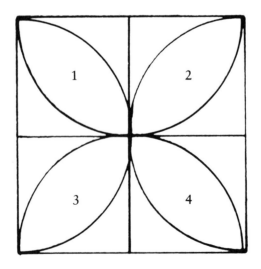

The template for this quilt is given on Plate 1.

Ribbon Quilt

SIZE OF QUILT

This quilt, measuring 80″ × 104″, is made up of forty-eight 12-inch pieced blocks set six in width and eight in length with a 4-inch border.

NUMBER OF PIECES TO BE CUT		AMOUNT OF MATERIAL
Piece No. 1 . . .	192	2 yards
Piece No. 2 . . .	192	2 yards
Piece No. 3 . . .	192	1 yard
Piece No. 4 . . .	192	1 yard
Piece No. 5 . . .	192	1 yard
Piece No. 6 . . .	192	1 yard

(Border pieces)
Two strips 4½″ × 80½″
Two strips 4½″ × 96½″   1½ yards

(Backing)
Two pieces 40½″ × 104½″   6 yards

COLOR CHART

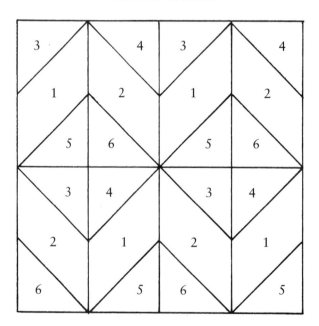

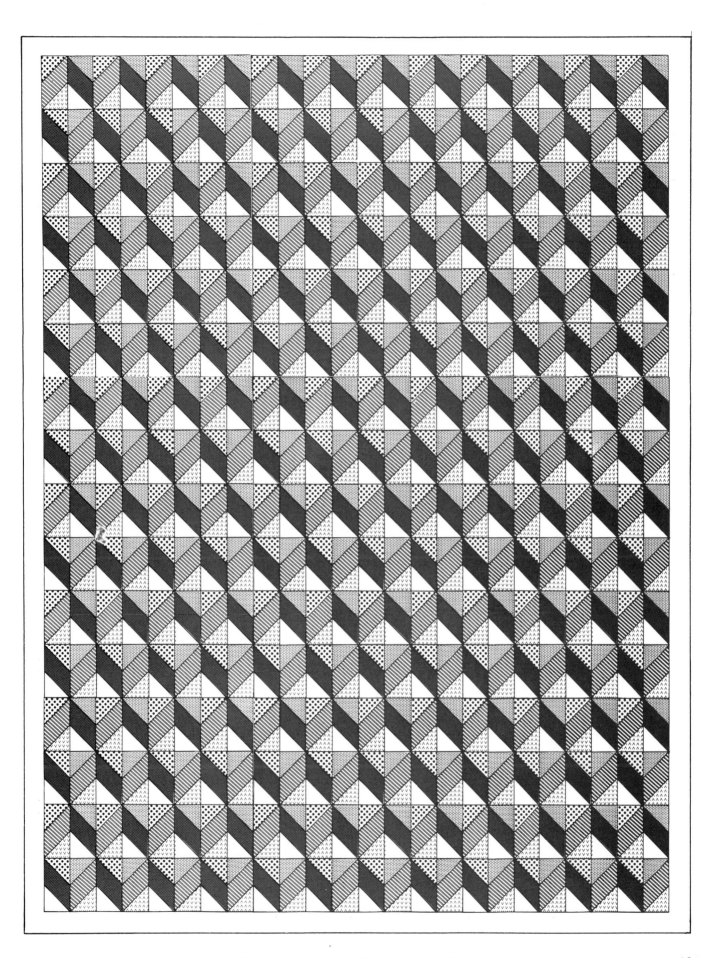

Templates for this quilt are given on Plate 2.

Crazy Anne Quilt

SIZE OF QUILT

This quilt, measuring 82″ × 102″, is made up of sixty-three 10-inch pieced blocks set seven in width and nine in length with a 2-inch inner border and a 4-inch outer border.

NUMBER OF PIECES TO BE CUT

	AMOUNT OF MATERIAL
Piece No. 1 . . . 126	1 yard
Piece No. 2 . . . 126	1 yard
Piece No. 3 . . . 126	1 yard
Piece No. 4 . . . 126	1 yard
Piece No. 5 63	½ yard
Piece No. 6 . . . 126	½ yard
Piece No. 7 . . . 126	½ yard
Piece No. 8 . . . 126	½ yard

(Inner border pieces)
Two strips 2½″ × 74½″
Two strips 2½″ × 90½″   1 yard

(Outer border pieces)
Two strips 4½″ × 82½″
Two strips 4½″ × 94½″   1½ yards

(Backing)
Two pieces 41½″ × 102½″   6 yards

COLOR CHART

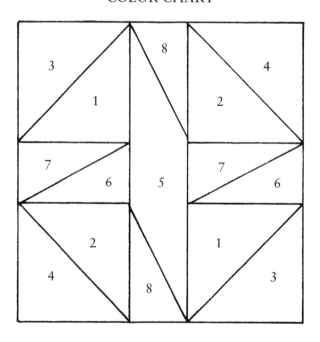

Templates for this quilt are given on Plate 3.

Windblown Star Quilt

SIZE OF QUILT

This quilt, measuring 80″ × 104″, is made up of forty-eight 12-inch pieced blocks set six in width and eight in length with a 4-inch border.

NUMBER OF PIECES TO BE CUT	AMOUNT OF MATERIAL
Piece No. 1 . . . 192	2 yards
Piece No. 2 48	½ yard
Piece No. 3 48	½ yard
Piece No. 4 . . . 192	1 yard
Piece No. 5 . . . 192	2 yards
Piece No. 6 . . . 192	2 yards
(Border pieces) Two strips 4½″ × 80½″ Two strips 4½″ × 96½″	1½ yards
(Backing) Two pieces 40½″ × 104½″	6 yards

COLOR CHART

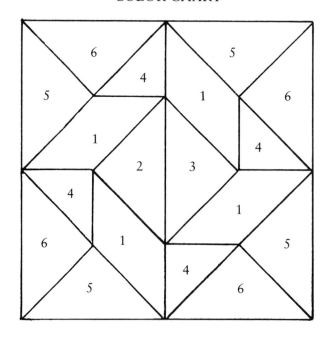

Templates for this quilt are given on Plate 4.

Virginia Quilt

SIZE OF QUILT

This quilt, measuring 80″ × 104″, is made up of forty-eight 12-inch pieced blocks set six in width and eight in length with a 4-inch border.

NUMBER OF PIECES TO BE CUT		AMOUNT OF MATERIAL
Piece No. 1	. . . 96	½ yard
Piece No. 2	. . . 96	½ yard
Piece No. 3	. . . 192	1 yard
Piece No. 4	. . . 96	½ yard
Piece No. 5	. . . 96	½ yard
Piece No. 6	. . . 192	1 yard
Piece No. 7	. . . 96	1 yard
Piece No. 8	. . . 96	1 yard
Piece No. 9	. . . 96	½ yard
Piece No. 10	. . . 96	½ yard
Piece No. 11	. . . 384	1 yard
Piece No. 12	. . . 48	1 yard
Piece No. 13	. . . 48	1 yard

(Border pieces)
Two strips 4½″ × 80½″
Two strips 4½″ × 96½″   1½ yards

(Backing)
Two pieces 40½″ × 104½″   6 yards

COLOR CHART

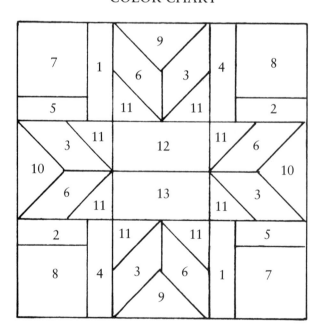

Templates for this quilt are given on Plate 5.

House on the Hill Quilt

SIZE OF QUILT

This quilt, measuring 80″ × 104″, is made up of forty-eight 12-inch pieced blocks set six in width and eight in length with a 4-inch border.

NUMBER OF PIECES TO BE CUT		AMOUNT OF MATERIAL
Piece No. 1 . . .	96	1½ yards
Piece No. 2 . . .	96	½ yard
Piece No. 3 . . .	96	½ yard
Piece No. 4 . . .	96	1½ yards
Piece No. 5 . . .	48	½ yard
Piece No. 6 . . .	48	1 yard
Piece No. 7 . . .	144	1 yard
Piece No. 8 . . .	48	½ yard
Piece No. 9 . . .	48	½ yard
Piece No. 10 . . .	192	1½ yards
Piece No. 11 . . .	48	½ yard

(Border pieces)
Two strips 4½″ × 80½″
Two strips 4½″ × 96½″   1½ yards

(Backing)
Two pieces 40½″ × 104½″   6 yards

COLOR CHART

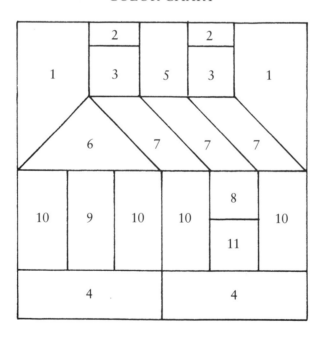

Templates for this quilt are given on Plates 6 and 7.

Bachelor's Puzzle Quilt

SIZE OF QUILT

This quilt, measuring 80″ × 104″, is made up of forty-eight 12-inch pieced blocks set six in width and eight in length with a 4-inch border.

NUMBER OF PIECES TO BE CUT		AMOUNT OF MATERIAL
Piece No. 1 . . .	192	1½ yards
Piece No. 2 . . .	192	1½ yards
Piece No. 3	96	1 yard
Piece No. 4	96	1 yard
Piece No. 5	48	½ yard
Piece No. 6	48	½ yard
Piece No. 7	96	½ yard
Piece No. 8	96	½ yard

(Border pieces)
Two strips 4½″ × 80½″   1½ yards
Two strips 4½″ × 96½″

(Backing)
Two pieces 40½″ × 104½″   6 yards

COLOR CHART

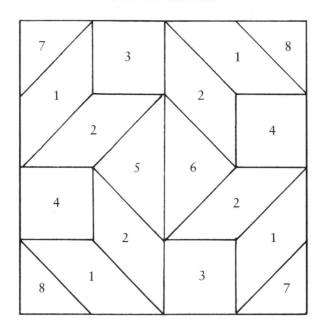

22

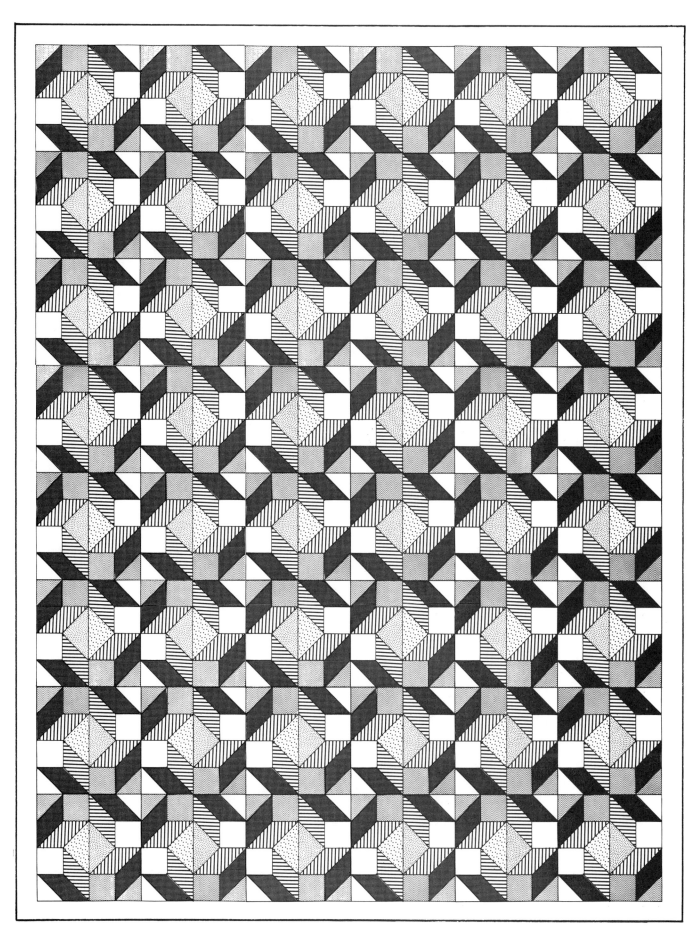

Templates for this quilt are given on Plate 8.

Swing in the Center Quilt

SIZE OF QUILT

This quilt, measuring 80″ × 104″, is made up of forty-eight 12-inch pieced blocks set six in width and eight in length with a 4-inch border.

NUMBER OF PIECES TO BE CUT	AMOUNT OF MATERIAL
Piece No. 1 . . . 192	1 yard
Piece No. 2 . . . 192	1 yard
Piece No. 3 96	1 yard
Piece No. 4 96	1 yard
Piece No. 5 . . . 192	1 yard
Piece No. 6 . . . 192	1 yard
Piece No. 7 . . . 192	1 yard
Piece No. 8 . . . 192	1 yard
Piece No. 9 48	1 yard

(Border pieces)
Two strips 4½″ × 80½″ — 1½ yards
Two strips 4½″ × 96½″

(Backing)
Two pieces 40½″ × 104½″ — 6 yards

COLOR CHART

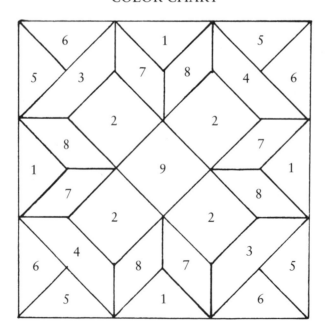

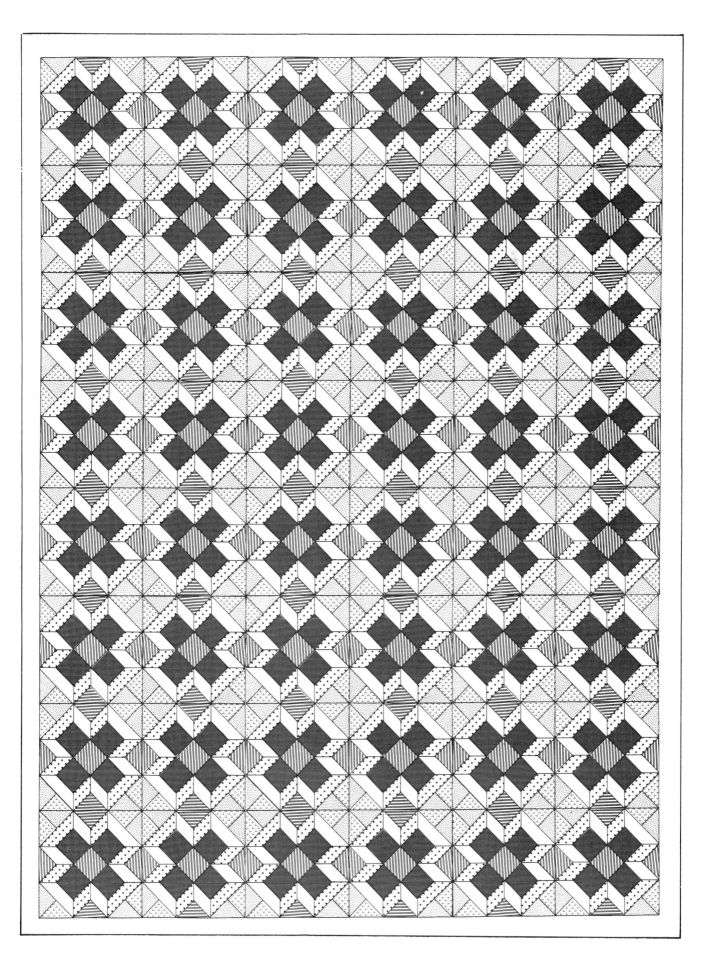

Templates for this quilt are given on Plate 9.

Weathervane Quilt

SIZE OF QUILT

This quilt, measuring 80″ × 104″, is made up of forty-eight 12-inch pieced blocks set six in width and eight in length with a 4-inch border.

NUMBER OF PIECES TO BE CUT		AMOUNT OF MATERIAL
Piece No. 1 . . .	96	½ yard
Piece No. 2 . . .	96	½ yard
Piece No. 3 . . .	192	1 yard
Piece No. 4 . . .	192	1 yard
Piece No. 5 . . .	192	1 yard
Piece No. 6 . . .	192	1 yard
Piece No. 7 . . .	96	½ yard
Piece No. 8 . . .	48	½ yard
Piece No. 9 . . .	48	½ yard
Piece No. 10 . . .	96	½ yard
Piece No. 11 . . .	96	½ yard
Piece No. 12 . . .	96	½ yard

(Border pieces)
Two strips 4½″ × 80½″
Two strips 4½″ × 96½″   1½ yards

(Backing)
Two pieces 40½″ × 104½″   6 yards

COLOR CHART

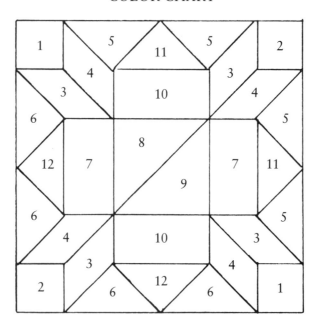

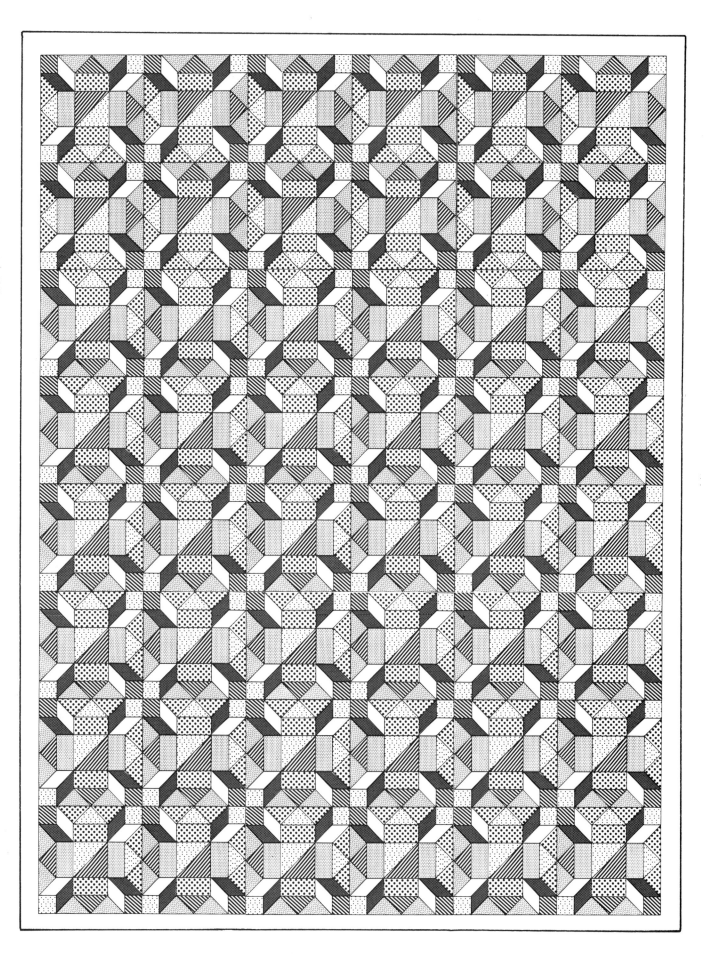

Templates for this quilt are given on Plate 10.

Many-Pointed Star Quilt

SIZE OF QUILT

This quilt, measuring 80″ × 98″, is made up of twenty 18-inch pieced blocks set four in width and five in length with a 4-inch border.

NUMBER OF PIECES TO BE CUT	AMOUNT OF MATERIAL
Piece No. 1 80	1 yard
Piece No. 2 80	1 yard
Piece No. 3 . . . 160	1 yard
Piece No. 4 . . . 160	1 yard
Piece No. 5 40	1 yard
Piece No. 6 40	1 yard
Piece No. 7 80	1 yard
Piece No. 8 80	1 yard
(Border pieces)	
Two strips 4½″ × 80½″	1½ yards
Two strips 4½″ × 90½″	
(Backing)	
Two pieces 40½″ × 98½″	6 yards

COLOR CHART

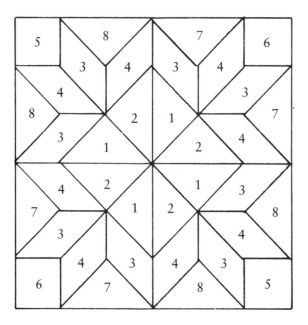

Templates for this quilt are given on Plate 11.

All Hallows Quilt

SIZE OF QUILT

This quilt, measuring 78″ × 94″, is made up of twenty 16-inch pieced blocks set four in width and five in length with an inner border of three inches and an outer border of four inches.

NUMBER OF PIECES TO BE CUT		AMOUNT OF MATERIAL
Piece No. 1 . . .	80	½ yard
Piece No. 2 . . .	40	½ yard
Piece No. 3 . . .	40	½ yard
Piece No. 4 . . .	80	½ yard
Piece No. 5 . . .	40	½ yard
Piece No. 6 . . .	40	½ yard
Piece No. 7 . . .	40	½ yard
Piece No. 8 . . .	80	½ yard
Piece No. 9 . . .	40	½ yard
Piece No. 10 . . .	80	½ yard
Piece No. 11 . . .	40	½ yard
Piece No. 12 . . .	40	½ yard

(Inner border)
Two strips 3½″ × 70½″
Two strips 3½″ × 80½″ — 1 yard

(Outer border)
Two strips 4½″ × 78½″
Two strips 4½″ × 86½″ — 1 yard

(Backing)
Two pieces 44½″ × 94½″ — 6 yards

COLOR CHART

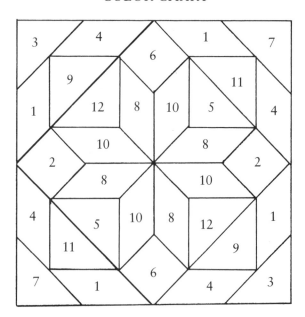

Templates for this quilt are given on Plate 12.

PATTERN PIECE FOR
ROMAN STRIPE QUILT

Allow for all seams when cutting.

ROMAN STRIPE
Pieces No. 1, 2, 3, 4, 5 and 6

PATTERN PIECE FOR
LAFAYETTE ORANGE PEEL QUILT

Allow for all seams when cutting.

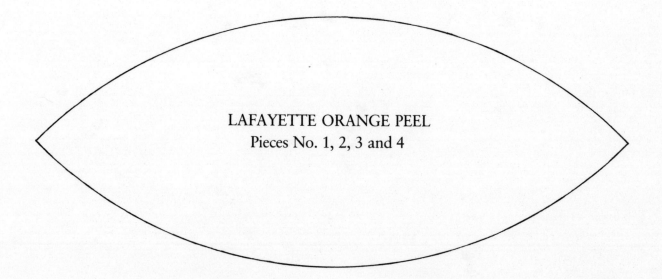

LAFAYETTE ORANGE PEEL
Pieces No. 1, 2, 3 and 4

Plate 1

PATTERN PIECES FOR
RIBBON QUILT

Allow for all seams when cutting.

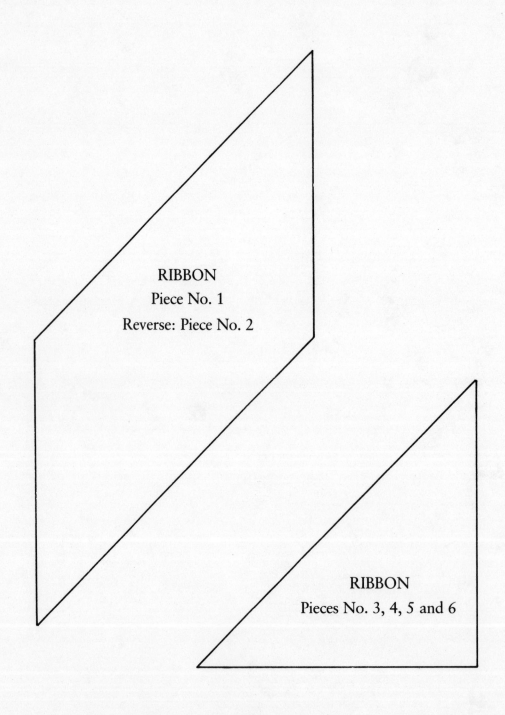

RIBBON
Piece No. 1
Reverse: Piece No. 2

RIBBON
Pieces No. 3, 4, 5 and 6

Plate 2

PATTERN PIECES FOR
CRAZY ANNE QUILT

Allow for all seams when cutting.

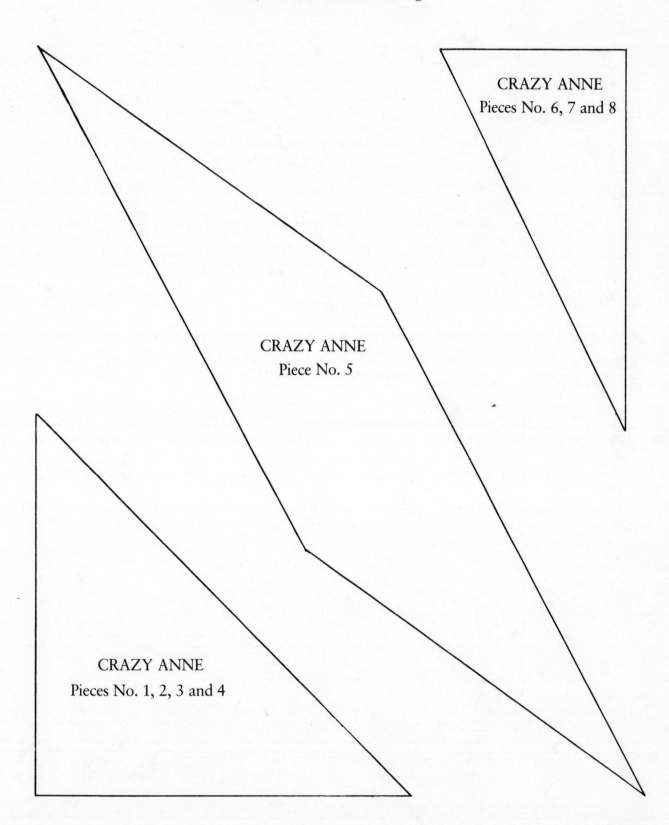

CRAZY ANNE
Pieces No. 6, 7 and 8

CRAZY ANNE
Piece No. 5

CRAZY ANNE
Pieces No. 1, 2, 3 and 4

Plate 3

PATTERN PIECES FOR
WINDBLOWN STAR QUILT

Allow for all seams when cutting.

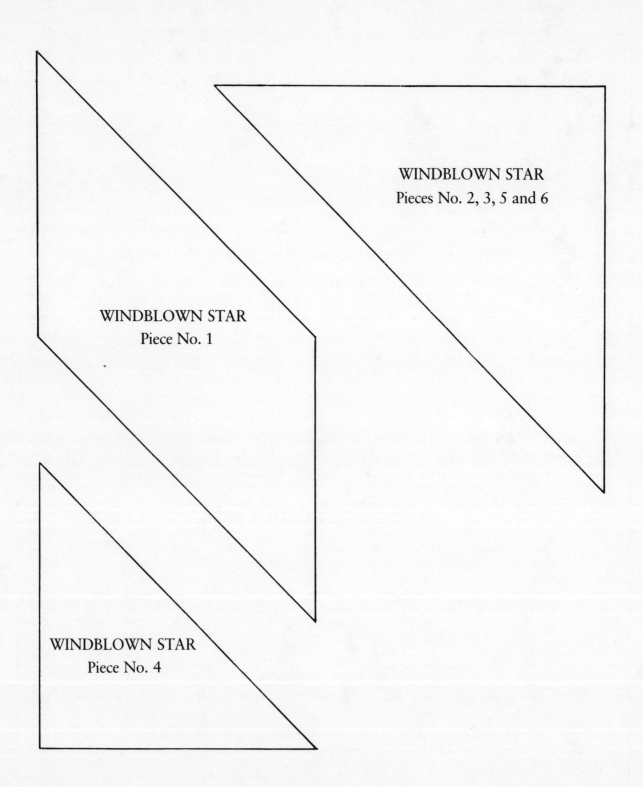

WINDBLOWN STAR
Pieces No. 2, 3, 5 and 6

WINDBLOWN STAR
Piece No. 1

WINDBLOWN STAR
Piece No. 4

Plate 4

PATTERN PIECES FOR
VIRGINIA QUILT

Allow for all seams when cutting.

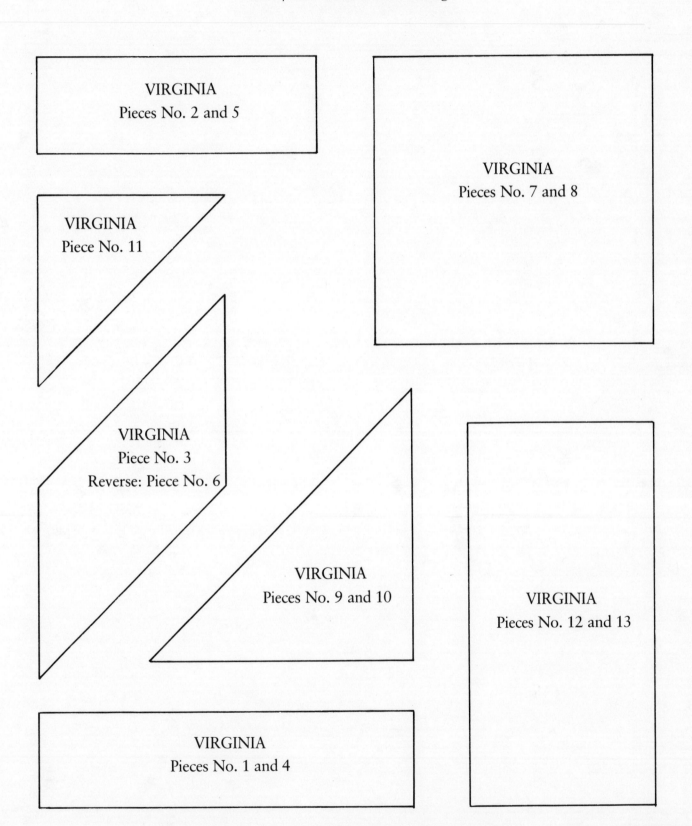

VIRGINIA
Pieces No. 2 and 5

VIRGINIA
Pieces No. 7 and 8

VIRGINIA
Piece No. 11

VIRGINIA
Piece No. 3
Reverse: Piece No. 6

VIRGINIA
Pieces No. 9 and 10

VIRGINIA
Pieces No. 12 and 13

VIRGINIA
Pieces No. 1 and 4

Plate 5

PATTERN PIECES FOR
HOUSE ON THE HILL QUILT

Allow for all seams when cutting.

HOUSE ON THE HILL
Piece No. 1

(Note: Cut half of these pieces
with template reversed.)

HOUSE ON THE HILL
Piece No. 4

HOUSE ON THE HILL
Piece No. 2

HOUSE ON THE HILL
Pieces No. 9 and 10

Plate 6

PATTERN PIECES FOR
HOUSE ON THE HILL QUILT

Allow for all seams when cutting.

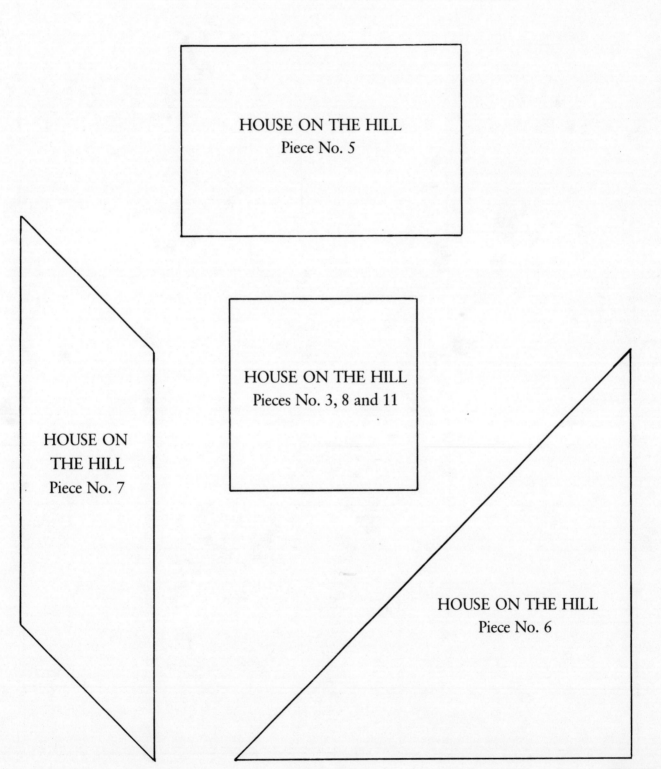

HOUSE ON THE HILL
Piece No. 5

HOUSE ON THE HILL
Pieces No. 3, 8 and 11

HOUSE ON
THE HILL
Piece No. 7

HOUSE ON THE HILL
Piece No. 6

Plate 7

PATTERN PIECES FOR
BACHELOR'S PUZZLE QUILT

Allow for all seams when cutting.

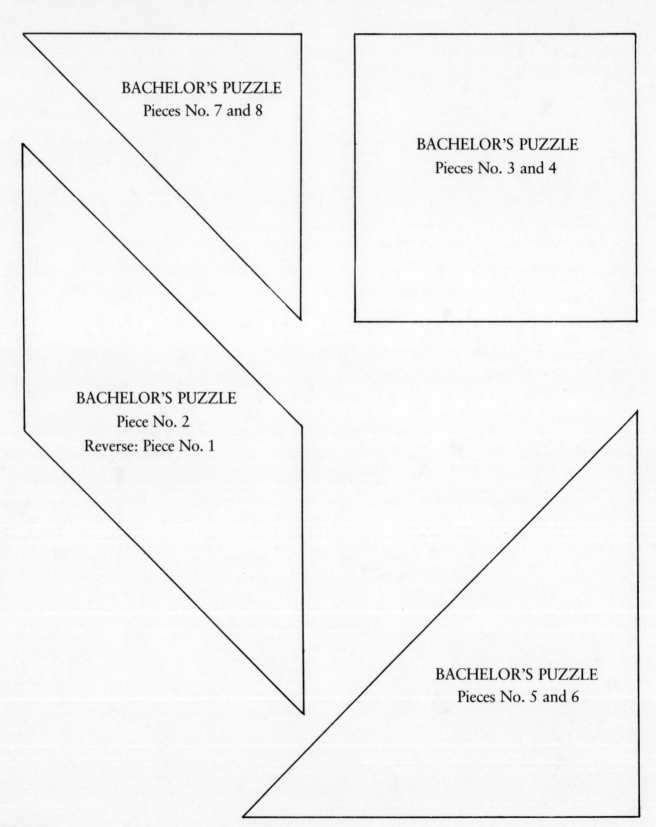

BACHELOR'S PUZZLE
Pieces No. 7 and 8

BACHELOR'S PUZZLE
Pieces No. 3 and 4

BACHELOR'S PUZZLE
Piece No. 2
Reverse: Piece No. 1

BACHELOR'S PUZZLE
Pieces No. 5 and 6

Plate 8

PATTERN PIECES FOR
SWING IN THE CENTER QUILT

Allow for all seams when cutting.

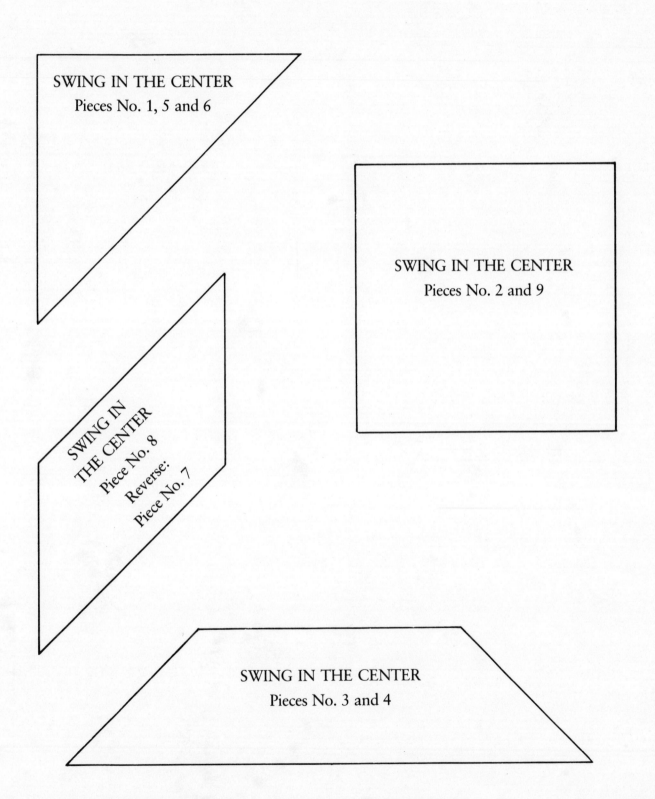

SWING IN THE CENTER
Pieces No. 1, 5 and 6

SWING IN THE CENTER
Pieces No. 2 and 9

SWING IN
THE CENTER
Piece No. 8
Reverse:
Piece No. 7

SWING IN THE CENTER
Pieces No. 3 and 4

Plate 9

PATTERN PIECES FOR
WEATHERVANE QUILT

Allow for all seams when cutting.

WEATHERVANE
Pieces No. 7 and 10

WEATHERVANE
Pieces No. 8 and 9

WEATHERVANE
Pieces No. 5, 6, 11 and 12

WEATHERVANE
Pieces No. 1 and 2

WEATHERVANE
Piece No. 3
Reverse: Piece No. 4

Plate 10

PATTERN PIECES FOR
MANY-POINTED STAR QUILT

Allow for all seams when cutting.

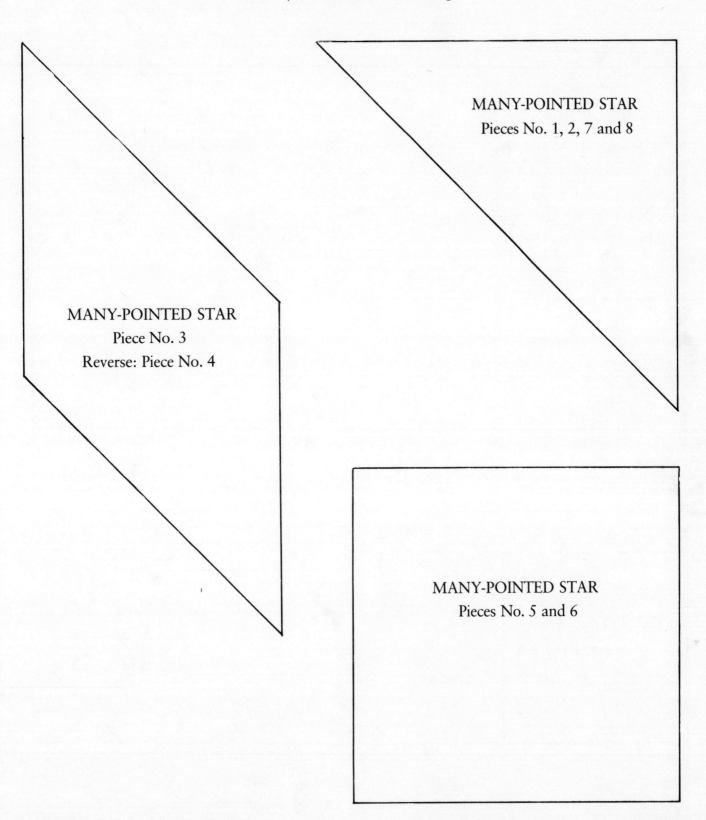

MANY-POINTED STAR
Pieces No. 1, 2, 7 and 8

MANY-POINTED STAR
Piece No. 3
Reverse: Piece No. 4

MANY-POINTED STAR
Pieces No. 5 and 6

Plate 11

PATTERN PIECES FOR
ALL HALLOWS QUILT

Allow for all seams when cutting.

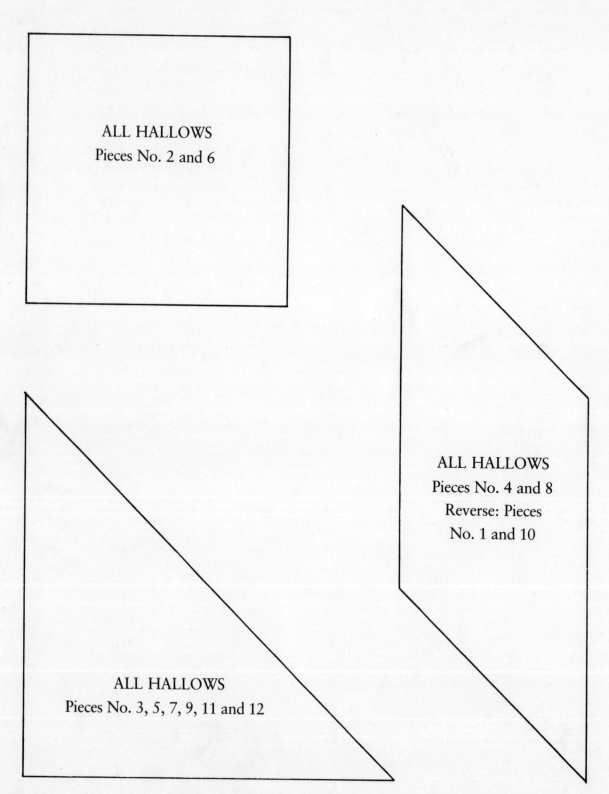

ALL HALLOWS
Pieces No. 2 and 6

ALL HALLOWS
Pieces No. 4 and 8
Reverse: Pieces
No. 1 and 10

ALL HALLOWS
Pieces No. 3, 5, 7, 9, 11 and 12

Plate 12